MAN RAY

BAZAAR YEARS

man
Ray.
Paris

MAN RAY
BAZAAR
YEARS

JOHN ESTEN

Introduction
Willis Hartshorn

RIZZOLI NEW YORK

FOR
CARMEL SNOW
ALEXEY BRODOVITCH

"We often speak of fashion influences.
Where do they come from?
Who sets them in motion?"
C. S.

OPPOSITE TITLE PAGE: "Augustabernard's new line. The gown billows
at the bottom." Photograph cropped as it appeared in Bazaar.
October 1934.

First published in the United States of America in 1988 by
RIZZOLI INTERNATIONAL PUBLICATIONS, INC.
597 Fifth Avenue, New York, NY 10017

ISBN 0-8478-1008-9
ISBN 0-8478-1009-7 (pbk.)
LC 88-43267

Book design by John Esten
Composition by David E. Seham Associates Inc., Metuchen, NJ
Printed and bound in Italy

**THIS BOOK IS PUBLISHED IN CONJUNCTION WITH
THE EXHIBITION MAN RAY/BAZAAR YEARS
ORGANIZED AND TOURED BY
THE INTERNATIONAL CENTER OF PHOTOGRAPHY, NEW YORK**

PREFACE AND ACKNOWLEDGMENTS

armel Snow once said "a well-dressed woman should have a well-dressed mind." For more than twenty-five years Mrs. Snow, the dynamic editor of *Harper's Bazaar,* not only dictated fashion trends but also influenced several generations of artists, writers, and photographers, among them Man Ray. Not a bad idea for the time!

In 1979, Mrs. Snow's niece and successor at "the *Bazaar,*" Nancy White, and I edited a book of photographs by Martin Munkacsi, the man who put movement in fashion photography. That book, as well as this one, grew out of the first-ever exhibition of the history of fashion photography, which was the idea of gallery director Robert Littman. At the time I was working at *Bazaar,* and Bob asked me to help with some of the photographers who had worked for the magazine. He wanted to include their work in an exhibition he was mounting at the Emily Lowe Gallery at Hofstra University in October 1975.

Imagine the audacity of it—fashion photographs exhibited in an art gallery! Always before, such photographs had been considered a means to an end—the end being fashion reportage and the eventual sale of clothing. Photography scholars had never considered fashion photographs very seriously (many still don't) in the history of the medium. That, however, did not stop director Littman!

The exhibition eventually included twenty-four photographers, many of whom were dead or long since forgotten. In some instances, the original work was unobtainable or had been lost forever but fortunately still existed in the pages of old fashion magazines. It was a major undertaking. It was a *very* good idea!

Among the "forgotten" photographers was one that had never really been forgotten—Man Ray. Everyone knew Man Ray as the great Dada and Surrealist painter, object-maker, and photographer. What most people did *not* know was that he also had been a fashion photographer. He had made fashion photographs only to support his other endeavors, but his genius carried through into this commercial work as well. The stunning results assembled here are of the photographs he made while working for "the *Bazaar.*"—what I call *Man Ray: Bazaar Years.*

Literally dozens of people have contributed to this project in many ways—some with scholarship, others with interest and enthusiasm, and still others with kindness and patience and time. I would like to acknowledge with sincere appreciation the following people:

Martin Schrader, publisher of *Harper's Bazaar* magazine, who with the Hearst Corporation, granted the rights to reproduce here and exhibit the Man Ray photographs that originally appeared in the magazine;

At the International Center of Photography: Cornell Capa, Executive Director; Anna Winand, Executive Assistant, Willis Hartshorn, Director of Exhibitions, who worked closely with me on this project and has written the illuminating introduction to the book; Lisa Dirks, Curatorial Associate; and David Spear.

Scott Hyde made the prints of the photographs for reproduction in the book as well as for the attendant exhibition; Paul Dzurella and his daughter Carol assumed the task of retouching the prints; Tom Kenny made the mechanicals; Charles Davey, of Rizzoli, oversaw the production and printing of the book.

John Tancock, of Sotheby's, offered scholarship and advice concerning Man Ray's work; Sidney Geist, who knows more about Brancusi than anyone else, verified several facts concerning the sculptor. Also helpful were Daniel Marchesseau, of the Musée des Arts Decoratifs, Paris; Merry Foresta, of the National Museum of American Art, Smithsonian Institution; Robert Kaufmann, Librarian of the Costume Institute Library of the Metropolitan Museum of Art; Sharon Brown, of the New York Society Library; and Debra Cohen, of *LIFE* Picture Service.

Juliet May Ray, the artist's widow; Jerome Gold, Administrator/Curator of the Man Ray Trust; and Theodore Feder, President of the Artists Rights Society, have been generous with their assistance in this project.

Providence Alongni, Brian Breger, Maggie Brown, Amanda Burden, Miki Denhof, Ann Edelstein, Richard Ely, Ron Levin, and Ray Roberts have greatly contributed to this project in various ways.

An especially grand thank-you to both Ruth Mueller and Mario Valentino, whose belief in this project as well as financial support helped make it a reality.

I am very grateful indeed to Stephanie Salomon, of Rizzoli, for her foresight and persistence in editing this book. Working with her was a continuous pleasure.

JOHN ESTEN

NOTE

The photographs reproduced here are cropped exactly as they originally appeared in the magazine. In some instances I have reduced the size of the prints to emphasize the framing Man Ray intended. (For example, page 17). I have tried to keep the tone of the magazine by using at least part of the caption that describes the people or the fashions in the photographs.

"Vionnet's crêpe [dinner dress] with a brooch of coral on the skirt." April 1936.

Poiret model posed in front of Brancusi sculpture *Maiastra*, ca. 1922.
Courtesy UFAC

INTRODUCTION

WILLIS HARTSHORN

On July 14, 1921, Bastille Day, Man Ray was welcomed to Paris by friends Marcel Duchamp and Francis Picabia and proclaimed America's "pre-eminent Dada artist." Five months after his arrival, Man Ray's first exhibition of paintings opened at Librairie Six. Although the exhibition was a successful Dada event, it was a financial failure. Disappointed at the response of the Paris art establishment, Man Ray decided to devote more of his energies to practical matters. "I now turned all my attention to getting myself organized as a professional photographer, getting a studio and installing it to do my work more efficiently. I was going to make money—not wait for recognition that might or might not come. In fact, I might become rich enough never to have to sell a painting, which would be ideal."[1] Man Ray began a photography business in his hotel room, a business that would successfully support his life as an artist until World War II necessitated his return to America.

Man Ray considered himself first and foremost a painter, though he was also a maker of objects, collage, films, and photographs. Art always had for him a strong element of playful exploration, and he constantly sought to expand the boundaries of what was aesthetically acceptable. This artistic curiosity, coupled with a practical sense of survival, made the commercial application of his talents a logical means of support. He was reserved about his commercial work, wanting to protect the supremacy of his art; still, he did not disparage it, for it allowed him to give time to more important things. Some of the Parisian Dadaists and Surrealists disapproved of Man Ray's commercial photographic activities. Unlike many members of the avant-garde, who came from wealth and privilege, Man Ray had to work for a living.

Born Emanuel Radnitszky in Philadelphia in 1890, and raised in Brooklyn, Man Ray gave up a university scholarship for the study of architecture in order to pursue his interest in painting. He supported himself with a series of jobs in commercial art, first as an engraver, then in advertising, and finally as a draftsman for a publisher of atlases. At the same time he frequented "291," the gallery run by Alfred Stieglitz. There he discovered work by Rodin, Matisse, and Cézanne, as well as by Pablo Picasso, Constantin Brancusi, and Francis Picabia, artists with whom he would later become friends. Fascinated by the European avant-garde, he quickly absorbed their lessons into his own painting.

Man Ray bought his first camera in 1914, believing he was better able to make effective reproductions of his own paintings than a professional photographer. He soon turned the camera into a means of earning money, taking portraits and photographing the work of other artists.

A year later, Man Ray met the French artist Marcel Duchamp, newly arrived in New York from Paris, who would become a close friend and influence. Duchamp, in the iconoclastic spirit of European Dada, had chosen to give up painting for an art that was more conceptual than pictorial. He conceived of the "readymade," or found object, to convey this Dada impulse. Pho-

Man Ray retouching a fashion photograph for *Bazaar*. Photographed by Roger Schall.
"Reporting Paris Styles." *LIFE* magazine, September 6, 1937.
Courtesy *LIFE* Picture Service

tography—modern, fast, and practical as well as a mechanical process that could be stripped of its artistic pretensions—fit well with his new regime. Beginning in 1920, Duchamp and Man Ray collaborated on a series of photographs documenting, among other things, Duchamp's Dada antics and his kinetic sculpture. Later, with Picabia, they published the only issue of *New York Dada*. When Duchamp and Picabia returned to Paris, they encouraged Man Ray to follow.

Man Ray settled himself in a Paris hotel room and began to photograph artworks and accept portrait commissions, as he had done earlier in New York. Most of the portraits were of artists and writers such as Ernest Hemingway, Salvador Dali, Jean Cocteau, Gertrude Stein, and James Joyce (photographed to promote his new book, *Ulysses*). Although these were largely unpaid commissions done to build a portrait file, it quickly became fashionable for the avant-garde to be photographed by Man Ray. While he continued to paint and participate in Dada and Surrealist events, these portraits first made his reputation.

Gabrielle Buffet, Picabia's wife, introduced Man Ray to the couturier Paul Poiret in 1922. Poiret had been using photographs to show his collection as early as 1911, when Edward Steichen photographed his models in the soft-focus Pictorialist style. This was a complete departure from the drawings that had heretofore dominated fashion illustration. Man Ray explains in his autobiography that Poiret had wanted "original pictures of his mannequins and gowns, something different, not like the stuff turned out by the usual fashion photographers . . . not the ordinary showing of gowns, but portraiture as well, giving more human qualities to the pictures.[2] Man Ray recounts with humor his first fashion assignment, which was plagued by his inability to speak French and by inadequate lighting equipment. To his relief, he found an American model with whom he could communicate and moved her to a favor-

ably lit location. "The room upstairs was flooded with sunlight from the windows; I would not need any other light. I had [the model] stand near the Brancusi sculpture [*Maiastra*], which threw off beams of golden light, blending with the colors of the dress. This was to be the picture, I decided; I'd combine art and fashion."[3]

Not only did Poiret encourage Man Ray to find new ways of dealing with fashion photography, but his assignment also inadvertently provided the artist with the "discovery" of the photogram technique, the results of which he would later name Rayographs. "It was while making these prints [for Poiret] that I hit on my Rayograph process, or cameraless photographs. One sheet of photo paper got into the developing tray—a sheet unexposed that had been mixed with those already exposed under the negatives . . . I mechanically placed a small glass funnel, the graduate and the thermometer in the tray on the wetted paper. I turned on the light; before my eyes an image began to form, not quite a simple silhouette of the objects as in a straight photograph, but distorted and refracted by the glass more or less in contact with the paper and standing out against a black background, the part directly exposed to the light. Tristan Tzara, champion of the Dada aesthetic, proclaimed these to be 'pure Dada creations, and far superior to similar attempts.' "[4] Poiret did not pay Man Ray for his fashion work, but he did give him a generous amount of money for two of his Rayographs.

Launched by his experience with Poiret, Man Ray received fashion assignments from other couture houses, including Worth, Chanel, and Schiaparelli. With his friend George Hoyningen-Huene, he produced a portfolio featuring some of the most beautiful women in Paris modeling jewelry and fashion accessories.[5] Through assignments for such periodicals as French and American *Vogue*, *Vu*, *Variétés*, *Jazz*, and *Vanity Fair* Man Ray's reputation flourished. Within a year of the artist's arrival in

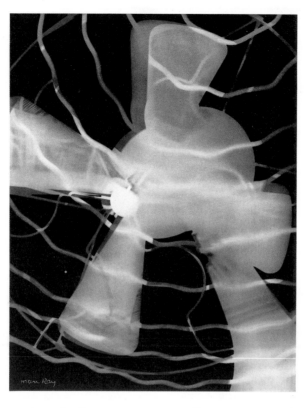

Le Souffle, 1931. Rayograph.
From the portfolio *Electricité.*
The Philadelphia Museum of Art.
Purchased:
Alice Newton Osborne Fund

Paris, *Vanity Fair's* editor, Frank Crownin-shield, had already published his portraits of Picasso and Joyce, and bought four Rayographs, which he then featured in the magazine.[6]

A portfolio commissioned by the Compagnie Parisienne de Distribution d'Électricité in 1931 offered Man Ray an excellent opportunity to integrate his work as an artist with a commercial assignment. For this work, depicting electricity and its applications, Man Ray used photograms along with photographs containing photo-grammed elements.[7] He would later use this technique in *Bazaar* to combine a photograph of a woman's legs with a photogram of a stocking. Man Ray preferred such commercial assignments to doing portraiture. "It was more irregular work, but better paying than portraits, leaving me more time for painting."[8]

The showings of the Paris couture houses of the 1930s dictated fashion trends, and America's apparel industry looked to Paris for the ideas and styles that filled the pages of New York magazines such as *Harper's Bazaar* and *Vogue.* From their Paris offices came the all-important photographs and drawings used to report the latest developments to their readers.

In 1932, William Randolph Hearst, publisher of *Harper's Bazaar,* the oldest fashion magazine in America, hired Carmel Snow away from *Vogue* in the hope of rejuvenating *Bazaar* with a "woman's point of view." Mrs. Snow initiated a series of changes that made the magazine one of the most succesful and innovative of its day. "I believe that a magazine must have surprises, I let myself go in flights of fancy that appealed to feminine readers. The surprises were at first the artists I introduced to our readers."[9] Mrs. Snow was quick to realize the value of talented people who may not have fashion experience but whose vision complemented her own. Almost immediately upon assuming editorship of *Bazaar,* Carmel Snow appointed Daisy Fellowes as Paris editor. Daisy, a wealthy Franco-American with influential connections in French social and artistic circles, was the perfect liaison for the magazine. She would work very closely with the artists and photographers in Paris, among them Man Ray.

"The Hon. Mrs. Reginald Fellowes
Our New Paris Editor."
Drawing by Jean Cocteau,
Bazaar, August 1933.

Another of Mrs. Snow's early appointments was graphic designer Alexey Brodovitch, a Russian exile who had recently come to America to establish a new department of advertising design—later called the Design Laboratory—at the Philadelphia College of Art. In his work Mrs. Snow "saw a fresh, new conception of layout technique that struck [her] like a revelation: pages that 'bled', beautifully cropped photographs, typography and design that were bold and arresting."[10] She invited him to join the staff of *Bazaar* as art director in 1934.

Brodovitch, who had been living in Paris for ten years, brought to *Bazaar* an enthusiasm for the work of the avant-garde. His European taste and sensibility changed the look of that publication, and in the end, the look of American magazines in general. Brodovitch's greatest contribution was in a new integration of type, picture, and the white of the page. He considered these elements not only on each individual page, but also as they flowed and harmonized from spread to spread throughout the magazine.[11] Mrs. Snow and Brodovitch both recognized that photography could be aesthetically and commercially exciting

at the same time. They supported and encouraged photographers to experiment and to show fashion as it had never been shown before.

It was through Brodovich that Carmel Snow remembers Man Ray coming to work for *Bazaar* in 1934. "Brodovitch still had commitments in Europe when he first came to the Bazaar and spent part of each year in Paris. He persuaded the avant-garde photographer Man Ray to make some of his strange, elongated compositions for us. Man Ray's impressions of the French collections were used, together with sketches by Bérard, for the first 'Fashions by Radio,' pictures transmitted from Paris directly by short wave, to appear in America. That was in September 1934."[12] For *Fashions by Radio* Man Ray used the Rayograph technique. Placing a piece of fabric and a paper cutout on top of the photographic paper, he gave the "photographic impression of a new fashion 'coming over' the short waves." Brodovitch's layout used type to further amplify the notion of a radio wave. Man Ray's second *Bazaar* image, an elongated silhouette, utilizes the exaggerated

Carmel Snow, editor *Bazaar* magazine, with Alexey Brodovitch, art director, discussing layout of the magazine. Bob Gerdy, managing editor, is behind Carmel Snow. 1952. Photograph by Walter Sanders, *LIFE* magazine © Time Inc.

perspective referred to by Carmel Snow, while showing little more detail than the Rayograph. Man Ray signed the work on the lower right, as if it were art.

In these first works for *Bazaar*, one can see how Man Ray substitutes imagination for the clearly defined rendering of clothes seen in the work of other fashion photographers. For Man Ray, the "impression" is more important than the accurate presentation of the product.[13] As in his art, the effect is often ambiguous and subtle. When editors encouraged Man Ray to make his pictures more "sexy," he explained that they were, if one knew how to look at them.

Man Ray brought his characteristic delight in experimentation to his work for *Bazaar*. There were no fixed boundaries between what he did for his art and what he did for commerce, and works were at times interchangeable. The nude used to illustrate a *Bazaar* article on the supposed benefits of ultraviolet light appears elsewhere in other formal variations. Here, a negative print, colored with violet ink at the time of printing the magazine, creates a variant unique to *Bazaar*. Similarly, he included some of his earliest fashion photographs of the mid

1920s in *La Révolution surréaliste*, the principal journal of the Surrealist movement.

Man Ray often turned to art to solve the problems of fashion photography. His painting *Observatory Time—The Lovers* was used as a background for a series of images, one of which appears in the pages of *Bazaar* with a model in a beach coat by Heim. In addition to using his own work, Man Ray also used sculptural elements commissioned from Alberto Giacometti. "During my period of fashion photography I disposed of a budget for backgrounds; I got him to make some bas-reliefs, units of birds and fishes which were repeated over a surface . . ."[14]

The work of Brancusi was also an inspiration, as in Man Ray's first pictures for Poiret, in which he decided to "combine art and fashion." The massive white forms used in three Bazaar photographs as well as the object paired with the model wearing Lanvin's white dress in another image strongly suggest a Brancusian influence. Man Ray identifies the prop in the Lanvin photograph as a "huge oak screw from a wine press which I had acquired recently in an antique shop with the idea of using it for a composition.[15]

In addition to such "found objects," friends often served as "found models." Nusch Eluard (the German actress Maria Benz), frequently modeled for Man Ray, and posed for a series of nudes he did for the book *Facile* in 1935, a collaboration with her husband, Surrealist poet Paul Eluard. Nusch also appears in *Bazaar* modeling Schiaparelli's Hindu-inspired gown and a Schiaparelli wedding dress. A *Bazaar* article written by Paul Eluard on an African art exhibit in Paris features a photograph of Man Ray's mistress, Adrienne, modeling an African-inspired hat.

Man Ray was the first and, for a time, the only Surrealist photographer, an association that is apparent in his work for *Bazaar*. At its best, Man Ray's fashion photography creates an atmosphere of dreamlike ambiguity and mystery. The model, as if a sculpture, is a cool and distant object staring expressionlessly into space. Hands, a favorite Surrealist fetish, are held stiffly, making the model appear as both a woman and a mannequin. Man Ray plays effectively with the ambiguities of the real and imagined implicit in the fashion image.

Salvador Dali's description of the Surrealist object applies well to Man Ray's fashion photography. "The Surrealist object is one that is absolutely useless from the practical and rational point of view, created wholly for the purpose of materializing in a fetishistic way, with the maximum of tangible reality, ideas and fantasies having a delirious character."[16]

The Surrealist style was soon adopted by other fashion photographers and dominated the pages not only of *Bazaar* but most other fashion magazines of the 1930s and '40s as well. The sexualization of Surrealist images and the "strangeness" of their aesthetic satisfied the public demand for novelty and were effective sales tools. It was through the power of mass publications such as *Bazaar* that the Surrealist sensibility was disseminated to an audience far larger than the followers of the avant-garde.[17]

The concept of a mass publication was not out of keeping with Man Ray's sensibilities as an artist. Since the beginning of his career, he had been more interested in the content of a work than in the form it took. He approached all media, whether painting, sculpture, or photography, as tools for the communication of his ideas. Discussing his painting *Observatory Time—The Lovers,* he admitted that he would have produced it as a color photograph if the technology had been available, "however rapidly I could paint, it was still drudgery after the instantaneous act of photography."[18] Man Ray had never been concerned with the uniqueness of the art object, and when it was lost, stolen or destroyed, he freely re-created it. Fearing the loss of *Observatory Time,* which had been stored in Paris during World War II, he promptly painted a copy. The ability to reproduce his art, as a preservation of his ideas, was most critical to Man Ray.

As a mass-circulation magazine, *Bazaar* offered the artist the ultimate multiple, along with an enormous audience for his work. However, Man Ray did not consider his work for *Bazaar* as art. He understood that work done for commerce could not reflect the complexity of his ideas. The marketplace was interested in appropriating the style but not the intentional shock

of Surrealism. Despite this, while living in Hollywood during the Second World War, Man Ray attempted to reconstruct his work for *Bazaar,* "I had none of the original prints of work I had done for the fashion magazines. . . . Making the rounds of second-hand bookshops, I went through back numbers, but most of my photographs had been cut out, evidently by students. This was very interesting; it confirmed my efforts to produce work that would have more than a transitory interest in contrast to the policy of the magazines which were interested in immediate news values, to be forgotten with the following issues."[19] While Man Ray lost interest in commercial photography at this time, clearly he came to prize his commercial efforts.

Man Ray's *Bazaar* years finally resonate like an archetypal Surrealist event, the chance meeting of two unlikely elements with unexpected and singular results. In this case, the disposable mass media and the quintessential avant-garde artist came together to produce images that indelibly transformed fashion photography.

■

"Vionnet's black silk organdie, shirred and cut till it becomes the ornament as well as the fabric." July 1936.

"Yrande's dark green cotton lace over pink." November 1936.

"Miss Eleanor Boardman wears a black satin evening dress from Mainbocher and over
  it a tailored tunic of red and gold lamé." November 1936.

"A Schiaparelli plum-covered velvet dinner suit, the skirt slit to the knee, the jacket
embroidered in irridescent purple and silver threads." Photograph cropped
as it appeared in *Bazaar*. January 1938.

"Suzy's black stitched taffeta sailor hat with a long silk tassel." February 1937.

"Brooding. Heavy. Black. Schiaparelli's magnificent cape emblazoned with gold."
January 1937.

"An idol's jewels, Eastern, rich." Cartier. August 1935.

"Molyneux's domino coat flowing profligately from the
shoulders in voluminous folds." March 1937.

"Instead of a tiara, a twist of diamonds dripping with rubies."
Model: Miss Barbara Cushing. March 1937.

"Madame Bourbon Patino, born in Spain and one of the most beautiful women in Paris,
dressed by Mainbocher in sapphire tulle and lace." February 1938.

" 'Chagrin d'Amour' is the name Chanel gives to this dress, in tulle dark as despair." The dress is photographed both front and back. July 1936.

"Molyneux's Madame Bovary: blackest silk organdie completely enveloping the arms and caught at the wrists." April 1937.

"The red badge of courage." Editorial feature illustrating the application of lipstick as "woman's gesture of courage in moments of stress." Photographic print with color added during the offset printing process. November 1937.

"Madness of the moment, Paquin's feather boa in all the colors of Harlem." Solarized negative print with color added during the offset printing process. February 1937.

"Knowing [the couturier, Poiret's] interest in so many arts, I brought my pictures of the nudes; he admired them very much, saying, a nude is always in fashion, pity . . . women cannot wear transparent clothes. Years later, I thought of this when I was photographing some filmy garments for the magazines." (Man Ray, *Self Portrait*)

––––––––––

"Beauty in ultra-violet." A beauty and health feature extolling the benefits of the recently invented ultraviolet lamp. Solarized negative print with color added during the offset printing process. October 1940.

"So end these twenty-four
hours—nightgown of sheer
transparent wool designed
by Olga Hitrova."
January 1936.

"Day begins—in a pale orange nightgown that Gorbatowsky slits to the waist in back."
January 1936.

"Pale, pink and fragile—Annek's nightgown. Add a slip and it becomes an evening dress." October 1936.

"Olga Hitrova's diaphanous gift to the evening in clear aquamarine." October 1936.

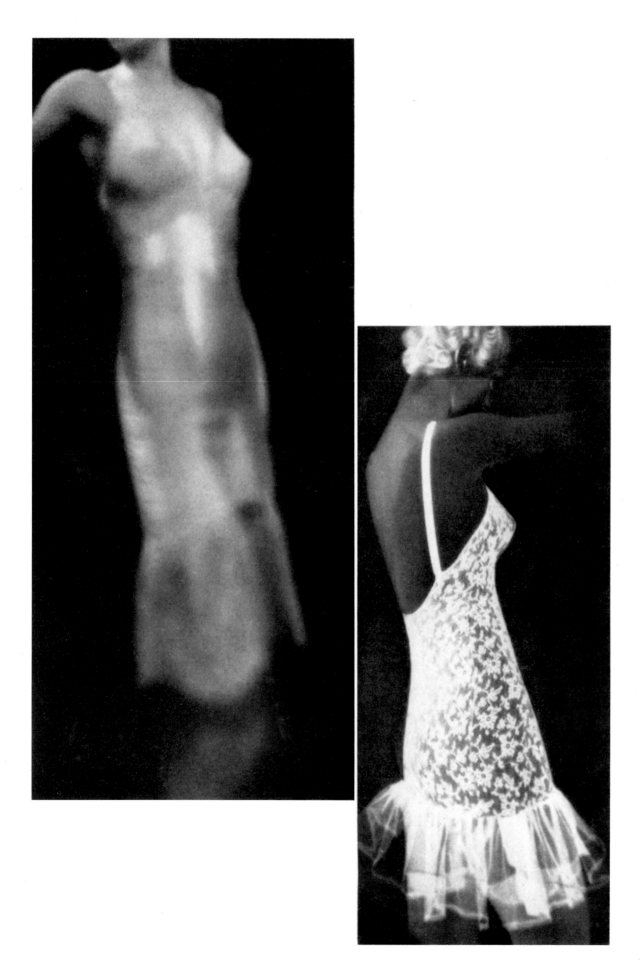

"The line we strive for—a smooth curve over the hips." Intimate apparel feature. September 1935.

"Miss June Presser of the Ziegfeld Follies."
Swimsuit feature. Photomontage. January 1937.

"Rise from bed like a mermaid in a sea-shell-pink chiffon
night gown." Gown by Annek. July 1937.

"Noël Coward's magnificent obsession: Miss Gertrude Lawrence. Norman Hartnell made the dress for Miss Lawrence's *Shadow Play* dance number—dusty pink tulle over pink satin." Photomontage. December 1936.

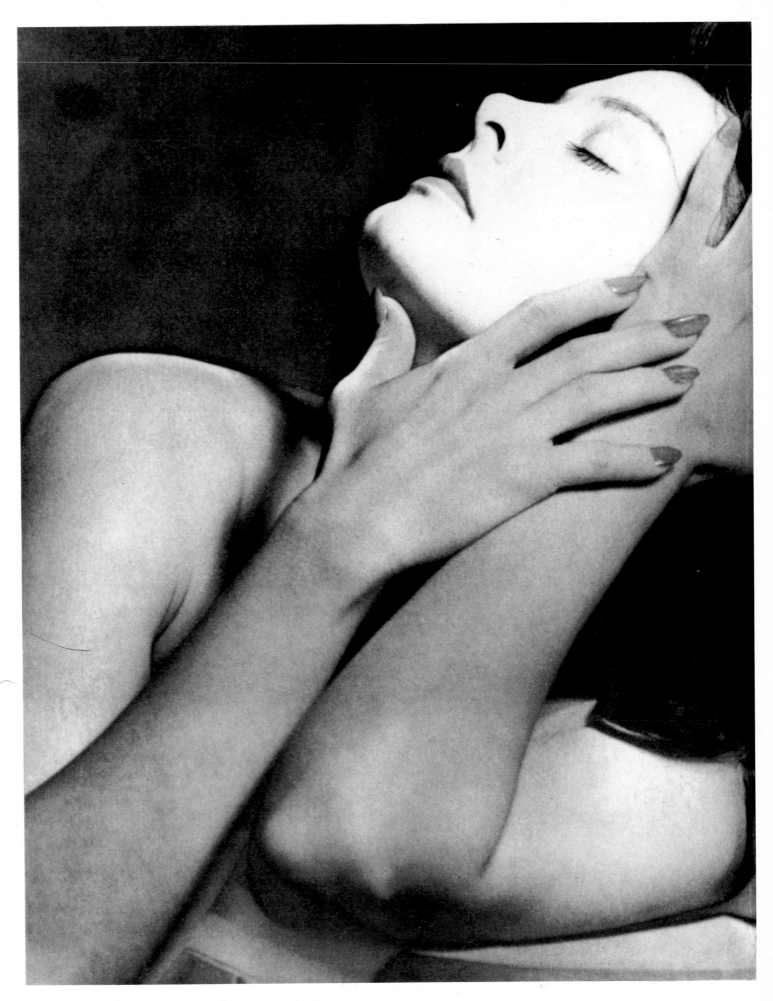

"We've all been to palmists and had them read our character in our hands. Make no mistake, out of the corner of the eye they size up our faces, too." Feature written by Elinor Guthrie Neff, beauty editor. October 1941.

49

"This young gray head. The glamour is spectacular in a way that the bewigged ladies of the eighteenth century understand very well. The secret is simple. White hair [lavender rinsed]." Solarized photographs. February 1937.

"Marie Laure, Vicomtesse de Noailles, muse of a circle of writers and artists in Paris." Solarized photograph. January 1937.
The Vicomtesse was descended from an illustrious literary background that included the Marquis de Sade, whose infamous memoirs were read by the Surrealists. Her maternal grandmother, Chévigné, was the model on whom Proust styled the Duchesse de Guermantes.

"Silken shadows. The darker, the sheerer." Photograph exposed with stocking Rayograph. October 1935.

"Paul Draper, following his brilliant display of tap dancing in the Corinthian Room of the Pierre [Hotel] with a partner wearing black silk satin, with high neck, skirt with fullness to the back." December 1936.

"Miss Mary Rogers, daughter of Will Rogers, in iridium-white lamé." December 1936.

"Schiaparelli's taffeta Pagliacci trousers in yellow with changeable orchid [colored] coat." January 1937.

Self-portrait of Man Ray in front of *Observatory Time—The Lovers*,
rue du Val-de-Grace, Paris, 1934.

This large canvas hung over Man Ray's bed in the rue du Val-de-Grace studio.
The painting was shown in the exhibition *Fantastic Art—Dada and Surrealism*, at the Museum of Modern Art in 1936.
After the exhibition it was displayed by Madame Helena Rubinstein in her Fifth Avenue beauty establishment
to promote a new lipstick. The painting was eventually returned to Man Ray
and was shown in the 1938 International Surrealist Exhibition in Paris.

"Against his surrealist painting 'Observatory Time—The Lovers,' Man Ray
photographs a beach coat by Heim of white silk painted with little brown foxes."
November 1936.

Observatory Time—The Lovers, 1932–1934. Oil on canvas. 39 x 98½ inches. Private collection.

"The exposition of Bushongo and Bankutu head-dresses at
the Charles Ratton Galleries in Paris will surely have a
happy influence on fashion." Hat by Lilly Daché. Feature
written by Paul Eluard. Model: Adrienne. September 1937.

"Maria Guy's garden-party hat of pale blue Panama
trimmed with hyacinths." Kodachrome.
June 1937.

"Man Ray, who has been painting in Hollywood, momentarily returns to his former medium, photography, with this extraordinary study of a woman's face for the beauty issue." November 1942.

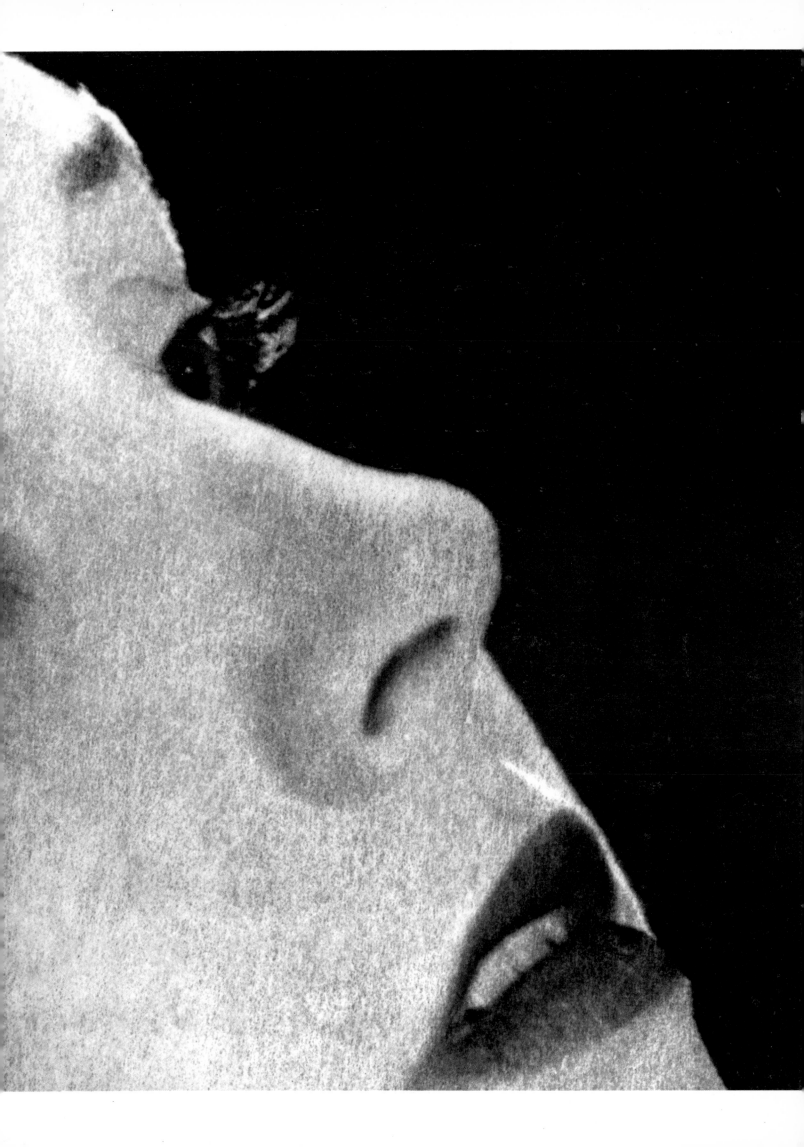

"Diamonds yellow as flame—not purely barbaric but splendid, mannered."
Designed by Madame Belperron. August 1935.

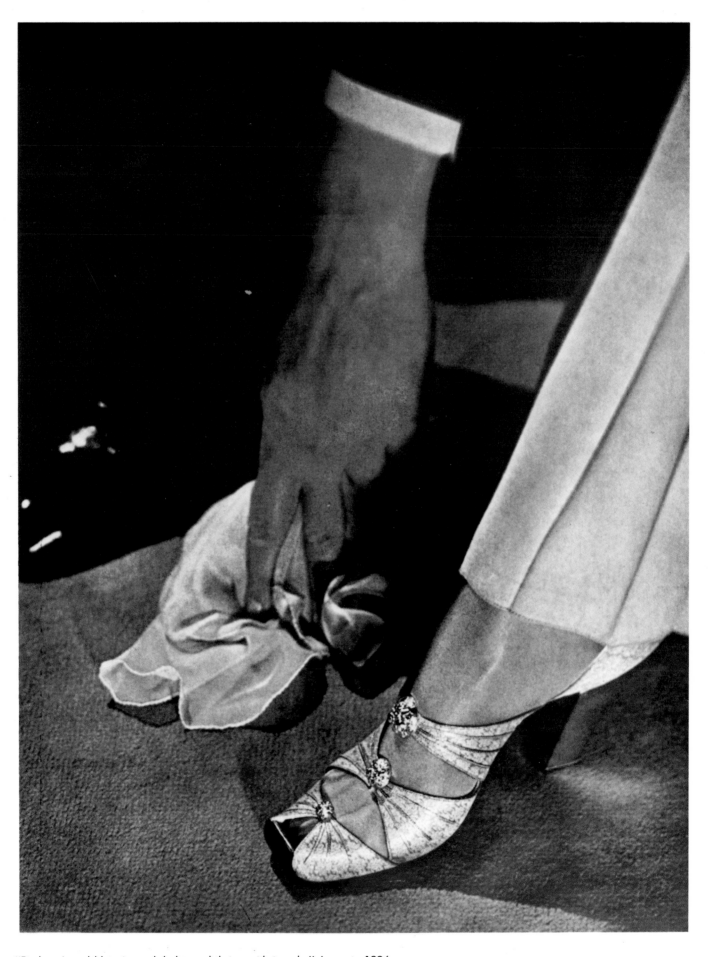

"Padova's gold lamé sandal clasped thrice with jewels." January 1936.

"Mainbocher bouquets—two flower prints." March 1936.

"Louiseboulanger—a new cut and a new white crêpe satin splashed with pansy browns and yellows." Print from multiply exposed negative. March 1936.

"Schiaparelli—stiff pink ducharne satin, cut Empire with a train."
Print from multiply exposed negative. March 1936.

"Alix has gone romantic, wildly, gloriously, with eighty-one yards of purple chiffon for the skirt and ten thousand Francs for the price. Ruching at the bottom in green, purple mousseline." March 1937.

"Chanel accents the bandaged waist with spreading skirts of tulle."
September 1937.

Three of the "birds" Man Ray commissioned the Swiss sculptor Alberto Giacometti to execute for use as backgrounds in the photographs on pages 77 and 79 can be seen hanging in the rue Denfert-Rochereau studio in Paris, 1940. On the balcony hangs the painting *Observatory Time—The Lovers*.

"The bolero appears again and again all throughout the Chanel collection."
September 1937.

"Black lace swallows flying all over the skirt of Vionnet's white organza." April 1937.

Brancusi's studio, 1925. Photography by Constantin Brancusi. Brancusi Archive,
Musée National d'Art Moderne, Centre Georges Pompidou, Paris.
Shortly after his arrival in Paris, Man Ray assisted the Rumanian sculptor in setting up a darkroom
in the studio, which enabled Brancusi to print his own photographs.

"Lanvin's classic white chiffon dress with stitched lamé around the neck and a curious belt made of
petals of the same material." November 1935.
The object photographed with the model is a wine-press screw found by Man Ray in a
Paris antique shop, and appears in the center of the above photograph behind
Brancusi's two *Endless Column* sculptures.

"Schiaparelli. 'Black tie,' the perfect printed black crêpe dress for little evenings." March 1936.

"Schiaparelli. Black skirt, pink plaid jacket and a soft felt derby inspired by [politician] Al Smith." March 1936.

The model at right, and in the two preceding pages, is posed with a base
of Brancusian design.

"Revillon's black Persian lamb coat and muff. A dark red felt fedora by Reboux."
November 1936.

"Mrs. Ernest Simpson, the most famous American in London, wears a Chinese dinner dress." May 1936.

"The pulse of fashion . . . by radio. A Schiaparelli in the new, romantic
Hindu mood." Model is Nusch Eluard, wife of the Surrealist poet
Paul Eluard. March 1935.

"The bride—Schiaparelli's dress of heavy white ribbed rayon ottoman."
Model: Nusch Eluard. Photograph cropped as it appeared in *Bazaar*. April 1936.

"Patou dinner dress of black crêpe trimmed with scalloped white organdie."
Background drawing by Man Ray. April 1940.

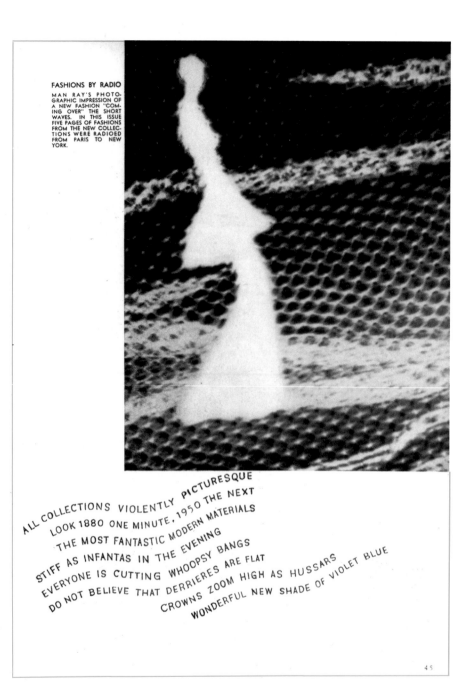

FASHIONS BY RADIO

MAN RAY'S PHOTO-
GRAPHIC IMPRESSION OF
A NEW FASHION "COM-
ING OVER" THE SHORT
WAVES. IN THIS ISSUE
FIVE PAGES OF FASHIONS
FROM THE NEW COLLEC-
TIONS WERE RADIOED
FROM PARIS TO NEW
YORK.

ALL COLLECTIONS VIOLENTLY PICTURESQUE
LOOK 1880 ONE MINUTE, 1950 THE NEXT
THE MOST FANTASTIC MODERN MATERIALS
STIFF AS INFANTAS IN THE EVENING
EVERYONE IS CUTTING WHOOPSY BANGS
DO NOT BELIEVE THAT DERRIERES ARE FLAT
CROWNS ZOOM HIGH AS HUSSARS
WONDERFUL NEW SHADE OF VIOLET BLUE

45

Tear sheet from *Bazaar* designed by art director Alexey Brodovitch.
September 1934.

Rayograph of newest fashion silhouette. This is the first
photograph by Man Ray to appear in *Bazaar*. September 1934.

"Serpent of the Nile—Alix's headdress in fibre net, with a silk jersey skirt and taffeta tunic."
April 1936.

"The slicker glorious, in strawberry-ice pink oilskin." Schiaparelli. June 1936.

"An idea from the Lowlands by Alix." May 1936.

"Mainbocher's triumph in black net with long tight sleeves." March 1936.

"Patou's languid white crêpe melting into pleats and swirled upward." February 1938.

"Schiaparelli evening dress made of a print like the flag of the Scottish Ogilvy Regiment."
March 1940.

Hatbox designed by Man Ray. "The most practical, hum-
drum, common-or-garden necessity of life can be beautiful, if touched by the hand of the artist." From a feature
on hatboxes decorated by contemporary artists.
March 1937.

NOTES

1. Man Ray, *Self Portrait* (New York: McGraw-Hill, 1963), p. 119.
2. Ibid., p. 122.
3. Ibid., p. 125.
4. Ibid., p. 129.
5. William A. Ewing, *The Photographic Art of Hoyningen-Huene* (New York: Rizzoli International Publications, Inc., 1986), p. 24.
6. Man Ray, *Self Portrait* (New York: McGraw-Hill, 1963), p. 176. Also see Sandra S. Phillips, "Themes and Variations: Man Ray's Photography in the Twenties and Thirties," in Merry Foresta, et al., *Perpetual Motif: The Art of Man Ray* (New York: Abbeville Press, 1988), pp. 196–97.
7. Jean-Claude Lemagny, and André Rouillé, eds., *A History of Photography: Social and Cultural Perspectives* (New York: Cambridge University Press, 1987), p. 122.
8. Man Ray, *Self Portrait* (New York: McGraw-Hill, 1963), p. 292.
9. Carmel Snow, with Mary Louise Aswell, *The World of Carmel Snow* (New York: McGraw-Hill, 1962), p. 100.
10. Ibid., p. 90.
11. Charles Reynolds, "Alexey Brodovitch," from the exhibition catalogue, *Hommage à Alexey Brodovitch*, Georges Tourdjman and Allan Porter, eds. (Paris: Ministère de la Culture, 1982), p. 119.
12. Carmel Snow, with Mary Louise Aswell, *The World of Carmel Snow* (New York: McGraw-Hill, 1962), p. 100.
13. Nancy Hall-Duncan, *The History of Fashion Photography* (New York: Chanticleer Press, 1979), p. 87.
14. Man Ray, *Self Portrait* (New York: McGraw-Hill, 1963), p. 252.
15. Ibid., p. 190.
16. Salvador Dali, *The Secret Life of Salvador Dali*, (1942), p. 312, cited in Arturo Schwarz, *Man Ray, The Rigour of Imagination* (New York: Rizzoli International Publications, Inc., 1977), p. 132.
17. Richard Martin, *Fashion and Surrealism* (New York: Rizzoli International Publications, Inc., 1987), p. 218.
18. Man Ray, *Self Portrait* (New York: McGraw-Hill, 1963), p. 254.
19. Ibid., p. 344.

SELECT BIBLIOGRAPHY

Ewing, William A., *The Photographic Art of Hoyningen-Huene* (New York: Rizzoli International Publications, Inc., 1986).

Foresta, Merry, et al., *Perpetual Motif: The Art of Man Ray* (New York: Abbeville Press, 1988).

Hall-Duncan, Nancy, *The History of Fashion Photography* (New York: Chanticleer Press, 1979).

Janus, et al., *Man Ray, The Photographic Image* (New York: Barron's, 1977).

Krauss, Rosalind, and Jane Livingston. *L'Amour fou: Photography and Surrealism* (New York: Abbeville Press, 1985).

Lemagny, Jean-Claude, and André Rouillé, eds, *A History of Photography: Social and Cultural Perspectives* (New York: Cambridge University Press, 1987).

Man Ray, *Self Portrait* (New York: McGraw-Hill, 1963).

Martin, Jean-Hubert, et al. *Man Ray Photographs* (New York: Thames and Hudson, 1982).

Martin, Richard, *Fashion and Surrealism* (New York: Rizzoli International Publications, Inc., 1987).

Penrose, Roland, *Man Ray* (London: Thames and Hudson, 1975).

Schwarz, Arturo, *Man Ray: The Rigour of Imagination* (New York: Rizzoli International Publications, Inc., 1977).

Snow, Carmel, with Mary Louise Aswell, *The World of Carmel Snow* (New York: McGraw-Hill, 1962).

Tourdjman, Georges, and Allan Porter, eds., *Hommage à Alexey Brodovitch* (Paris: Ministère de la Culture, 1982).